The "S" Word

A Suicidal Mind

MELISSA F. NEWBY

outskirts press

In dedication to those who have lost their fight,
who have fought, and are still fighting suicide.

Table of Contents

Part 1

The "S" Word

SOMETIMES I THINK about it. The "S" word. Actually, I always think about it. I wonder what people would think if they knew. Would they try to help? Or would they still turn their heads as they do now? Looking the other way to not get involved in such ridiculous matters.

Life is funny. If you're not in the in-crowd, then you're really nobody at all. You don't belong. There's no place for people who don't fit with what society portrays as perfect. You might as well give up and let go. Give in to the "S" word.

I'm thirty-seven years old and I feel stuck. Stuck in a world where no one really understands me or cares to even try. I feel alone. As if everyone and everything around me is moving, but I'm stuck standing in one place. Out of place. There's constant noise, but I can't make sense of it. I can see, but I can no longer comprehend. I can't move. I'm just ... stuck.

I want to live and breathe. To be happy. I don't want to walk around feeling broken and caught in the despair of my own loneliness. I want to break free, but I can't. I don't know how. It's not something I can just turn off, rewind and start over. I can't. It's impossible.

I see people around me staring. Can they see the hurt inside of me? Is it noticeable? Why don't they help me! If only one; one single person. A smile, an arm, a hand. Just reach out to me. Tell me, it'll be alright. That I'll be alright. Tell me, "I see you. I hear you. I know. I'm here."

I play the "S" word out in my mind. I contemplate the different ways it could happen. The anti-depressants in my bathroom medicine cabinet. The rope hanging in the garage, or the chef's knives perfectly aligned in the kitchen. Yes, I've thought and imagined all of it.

A crippling fear strikes my heart and sends a flood of tears falling from my eyes. I don't want the "S" word to consume me. I don't want it ripping me apart like a pack of hungry wolves fighting over a piece of meat. I don't want the "S" word taking me from this world, but it's all I can think about.

How wonderful the end could really be. No more feelings. No more loneliness. No fear of constant rejection. Most importantly, the "S" word no longer taunting me. There would be nothing. Just quiet, stillness, everlasting and eternal peace.

The world has painted a glorious picture of what perfect should be; but it's all a lie. There's no room for the rejects, the losers or the outcasts. There's only room for the well-known and the well liked. If you're not in either one of those circles, you mean nothing to no one.

Day after day I dream about the "S" word. What

if I completed my mission? What if I didn't? What if someone stepped in and stopped me. What if?

Who would really come to my funeral? What words would they choose to speak? Would anyone cry? Would there be whispers echoing through the halls? Would there be anybody that wished they had reached out? Surely, they saw the pain I was in.

I look at myself in the mirror and don't recognize that girl anymore. I see her eyes, her lips, her skin, the color of her hair; but I don't know her. The real me inside is gone. It has been replaced by another. One swallowed up whole by the "S" word.

Pretending is how I manage. I masquerade as one who is happy, but it's simply a mask. A painted face I wear. But if someone were to wipe the makeup off and remove this mask, then he or she would be able to see the real me. The lost, scared and empty soul I really am. The girl, whose hope is fading. The one who is being overtaken by darkness.

You may ask, "What has caused you to be this way?" I don't know. I don't have the answer for you. I want to be free. I don't want to dwell on the "S" word. I don't want it running scenes through my mind, casting me as the leading role whose ending is tragic. Yet, I can't seem to find my way out of this madness.

I hate going out in public and despise being

around others. The fake smiles make me nauseated, and it only pushes me towards the "S" word that much faster. I don't mean to be like this; but I can't stop thinking about it.

The "S" word. What if? Just maybe I could find solitude in going away forever. Forever. Never coming back. What if?

What could possibly be a better solution than staying in a world where I don't fit? I'm not liked. When I could simply disappear and no one would ask why. They may think "Oh, that's sad," but then go right back to their busy lives. As if it didn't matter either way. What is the point of staying in a world like that?

I've tried to make my life better. I put myself through college and earned a master's degree in business management. I have a great career at Kirk and Goble as a marketing manager for eco-friendly products. I'm still young with a full life of opportunity ahead of me. But I'm not happy. I'm sad and depressed. It's eating away, to the very core of my soul. I am drowning in the "S" word.

Most days I get up longing for it. Praying to be brave enough to see it through. I sit and allow the world around me to crumble because I've lost all hope. Oh God, how I want this torture to finally end!

The people I work with don't see. They can't.

They won't let themselves. They walk past me in hopes to avoid any conversation. They don't make eye contact. It's okay though. I understand. No one knows how to help the wounded, the ones that don't belong, the distressed or the lost. Those who are hopeless, allowing the "S" word to consume their whole life.

At times I feel like a trapped prisoner trying so desperately to escape the trickery of my own doings, but I'm in a deep pit that I can't rise from. There's no ladder to climb up or no door to open. There's no hidden passageway. Only darkness. It's dark and cold and I'm alone. My body is plunged beneath the water and I can't breathe. I can't swim to the top. I feel the "S" word closing in slowly and tightly.

Then suddenly, a gasp of air and I'm back in the real world. The world that doesn't accept anything less than perfect. The world I no longer want to be a part of. Why did I have to breathe again?

I didn't choose this path. Who would?

A few years ago, I felt normal. I knew what I wanted in my life. I had dreams to achieve. Being introduced to this "S" word is something I would have never wanted for my life. Being without purpose and drifting far away from what should matter. Separated, cut off, and all alone. Lost in misery. I used to be happy. Very, very happy. I remember laughing, a lot. But somewhere in the middle of it all, the disappointments of life entangled me in their dark webs. I find myself no longer caring about my appearance. My hair is pulled back into a tight bun. My clothing is loose and unflattering to my body. My skin is pale and dry. I no longer hide the blemishes with makeup. My body is no longer slim. I work long hours to not think about the "S" word, but it always creeps into my thoughts and destroys my mind.

During the brief silent moments I have to myself, I think of new ways to give in. To end this life and to finally let go. It's only in those moments, I find true sanctuary. A bliss of knowing how close I really am. For a moment, I'm the one in control.

At night, I lie awake staring at the ceiling. I wonder if tomorrow I'll somehow find the courage to embrace death and welcome it without hesitation. But, somehow morning would come and I'd find the strength to get up, get dressed and go to work.

There's no rhyme or reason as to why I feel this way. No fault to anyone. I simply exist to be existing. I breathe in and out to make it through the day.

I don't want to hurt anyone. I never intended for people to feel sorry for me or pity me. I just wanted to be accepted, to be liked, to have a hand that's willing to lift me up when I fall. I wanted someone to perceive that I'm not alright. I haven't been for a very long time. I needed someone to pull me out of the shadows. I needed help. Someone who could see all the pain that I've bottled up inside. Someone who was willing to listen to my story. Someone who I could trust and believed that I can make it.

Can anyone see me or hear my desperate pleas? Is there anyone who's willing to step up and help me? My body and soul are tired of pretending that it's all okay. That I'm okay. I am not. My spiritual being is literally crying out, begging for someone to help me.

I can feel the waves of the ocean crashing around me and my body struggling to keep afloat. My head is barely above the water. Could I be so brave to let myself just sink to the bottom and then drift ashore to be laid to rest once and for all?

Some people would say "Shake it off;" but I can't. How can I? How can I shake the "S" word when it's the one thing taking over my mind, my thoughts and my feelings? They're not the ones in pain. They don't get it. How could they?

Life is strange. One moment you're happy, even on top of the world. The next moment you're not. You're at the very bottom trying hard to reach the top once again. You just want to be normal. Although people try to tell you to snap out of it, you can't. How can you snap out of something that put you there without your consent? There's no magic pill for happiness. I know. I've tried and looked for it. It doesn't and has never existed.

The "S" word is now a part of me. I can't loosen its grip. It doesn't go away. It's always with me.

I don't sleep much anymore. The dark circles under my brown eyes are becoming more and more apparent. I only sit in my office and pretend to work on things that no longer matter to me. I find that I'm wanting nothing to do with the life that surrounds me daily.

I try very hard not to think about what the "S" word has in store, but I can't. I see the script that's laid out before me and I'm overwhelmed with curiosity.

I've heard it said that the best way to go is through water. Drowning is peaceful and it's quick. Your body goes into an unconsciousness state as the air is cut off. Then you just go to sleep.

Stop it, I tell myself. *Stop being like this.* But my head doesn't listen. I don't want to keep living like this. Like a caged animal just waiting to finally die. Just pleading and begging for death to come. And it never does.

I wish I could explain to you why or how the "S" word came into my life. How it took over and never let go. I wish, at times, it would go away, but then I would truly be all alone. Maybe you'd know how to help if you could see all the pain it causes, all the anger, all the hurt, all the confusion. You could stop it. You could save me.

There were days when I wished to feel absolutely nothing. To allow all the crippling brokenness to just take over. *"This is what I want; this is what I need,"* I'd whisper to myself to make it seem better than it actually was.

I never wanted to be considered weak or cast aside from everyone and everything. I never wanted to be the girl that you avoided and constantly ignored.

Happiness is what we all desire in some way or another. It's what I want; to be happy. Really happy. I want to have a zeal for life and the will to be strong. To believe that my life has a greater purpose. That I belong, I'm liked and accepted.

I signed up for online dating. Thinking that by throwing myself at men, I could be happy. That the depression, the sadness that gorged my life would slowly slink away and I'd be free to experience the world as a girl who belongs. Unfortunately, the more I threw myself, the more hurt I felt. Through the hurt, I became guilty and ashamed that I sunk so low in my life to be someone I'm even more disgusted with.

I feel my mind has been twisted, and my soul warped. The battle of being here, alive, in a world I never asked to be a part of is becoming tiresome. I need to feel freedom and my body needs to rest.

Surrendering to the victory of death is what I need to do. Then can I truly win. So, I think.

Don't ask me to explain my reasons to you. I can't. I wouldn't know how to make you fully comprehend what the "S" word has done to me or why I can't stay in this world. I'm falling apart slowly. My world is unraveling beneath my feet. I can't keep standing on this ground which is no longer solid and safe for me. Not by myself.

If someone, anyone could reach me. Wrap their arms around me, hug me, love me, and tell me that this is all a part of life. That I can get past this. Tell me, "I'll help you through it. Just lean on me and we'll come out of this together."

Someone! Please help me! Anyone?

Please hear the cries that have been silent and feel the pain that's buried. See that inside, I'm dying. The "S" word has bound me as its captive and it will not let go. I need you to see me and to save me. My spirit has been broken, my body worn out, and my mind disorientated. My soul is unable to find its way back to the light. Suicide is my only option now. It's what I must do.

My name is Alison Winters and this is the story of how I killed myself.

PART 2

Leading Up To

SUICIDE IS LIKE a cancer. It starts off small. Very small. Untraceable in fact. But day by day it grows. It'll begin to fester in ways which cannot be explained. It causes anxiety, depression and the cravings for death. Your body, your mind, your soul, they no longer belong to you. You become a prisoner in a prison that you created.

I remember that day as if it is something I must relive every day. A tiny memory embedded in the back of my mind to replay forever. A haunting moment in time. One that I will always think of. The sun was hidden behind a small cluster of clouds, and the world was silent. I could smell the rain before it even began to fall. A light roar of thunder in the far distance began to rumble. I felt confident in my decision and there was no turning back. Not this time.

It was a Wednesday late afternoon. I had left work earlier than usual, using the excuse of not feeling well. It was a lie. I was fine. But I needed to be home. I needed to clean and get everything ready for that night. I needed to prepare for the last night of my life.

Just one quick stop before heading home that day. A stop I was already dreading to make, the United States Post Office. I had a letter to mail and it could only be mailed on this day.

When I reached the post office, I stepped out of

my white Grand Jeep Cherokee, pulled the letter from my pocket and began walking towards the mailbox drop. My hands began shaking with every step I took and for a split second I thought about turning around.

I opened the mailbox drop, took a deep breath and closed my eyes as a slight hesitation crawled up the back of my spine. I knew the contents of this letter would ensure a painful greeting. My eyes opened. I let go of the letter and listened as it fell inside. I'll never forget the sound. The light thump vibrated in my ears as it dropped. It was done.

I turned around and got back into my car. This was it. I sat in silence the whole twenty-five minute drive back to my apartment. No music. No talk radio. Just me. Lost in the maze of my own thoughts.

The world will go on without me, as if I never entered in. The world will be better off. It'll be lessened by one person who's just taking up space. I have become numb. I'm empty, physically and emotionally drained. I'm invisible. I know I will not be remembered. I will be yet another headstone lying in a cold grave that's never visited. My name will be forgotten. You don't see it. You never did. Me. On the verge of absolute explosion. But now, I'm here, standing on the edge. I've been waiting and now I'm ready to make the final jump.

It seemed I had been in the car only seconds

before pulling into the parking lot. Unbuckling my seat belt, with my heart beating fast, I had to remind myself, *breathe in, breathe out. Breathe in, breath out. You're almost there.*

Meticulously I planned this night down to the very last detail. Everything was perfect. It had to be. At exactly 8:45 p.m., my heart will stop beating. My body will lie in a stiff cold, my mind will be blank, and my soul will finally be free of this fatal torment. Tonight, I'm surrendering to the curse that longs for death. Tonight, I'm giving in to suicide.

The lavender scents filled the air as I began scrubbing every inch of my apartment. I didn't want there to be a smudge of dust or even a pillow out of place. I folded the laundry from this morning, vacuumed the carpet, mopped the hardwood floors in my kitchen, put the dishes away, and took out the trash. Looking around, I felt accomplished. I know what you're thinking, *don't do it.* Why not? When the truth is you never said anything to me. You never once caught on and realized what I was battling. Did you choose not to, or did you not know how to help me or what to say to someone like me? I guess we'll never know.

All would be fine. At last. I know this is what I'm wanting. It's all I've ever wanted for the last couple of years. And now I'm finally brave enough to see it through to the end. It's a funny kind of feeling inside of me because I never thought I could do this, but here I am and everything's going according to plan.

Over the past couple of weeks, I sat on my back balcony and contemplated how I was going to do it. At first, I thought about leaping to my death from this very balcony. Let my body fly and allow gravity to pull me down to earth. I quickly dismissed this idea because I didn't want my body smacking hard onto the pavement and somehow survive the fall.

My second thought was to slit my wrists in the bathtub. Surround myself in my own blood. Feel the pain and watch as the life inside leaves my body. Let my body sink down into the bathtub and become just a blur, but I couldn't. I didn't want my mom or my dad to witness that. It would be too much for them. They wouldn't be able to cope. My third thought was to purchase a handgun in the next town over. I would sit on the couch, close my eyes and pull the trigger. *What if you miss?* I thought. *What if it hurts?* I wondered. I finally said no to this notion because of the blood splatter on the walls and couch, and the loud sound the gunshot would make. *I don't want to feel any pain,* I told myself. I want to die peacefully, quietly and without disfiguring my body. Then I thought of the absolute perfect way for me to end it all.

Sipping on my glass of red wine, a small smile

came across my moist lips. I smiled because tonight was the night I'd stop living. Stop feeling like I'm the odd one. Stop seeing that there's no one in my life who cares about me. Tonight, everything would just stop.

The buzzing of my cellphone interrupted my thoughts. It was my mom. *Weird*, I thought. She never calls me this late. I couldn't answer though. I dared not to. I knew if I did, I wouldn't be able to go through with my plans. I'd postpone. Again. I couldn't have any distractions. Not this time. *Sorry mom,* I thought, and turned off my phone completely.

PART 3

A Visit from Death

WALKING INTO THE bathroom, I stood in front of the mirror, just gazing. I needed to see all of me. I pulled my long brown hair out of the tight bun I had been wearing all day. For a moment, I felt scared. I quickly brushed that feeling aside as soon as it had come. Nothing was going to get in the way. Nothing.

Plugging in my iPod, I set the music to classical piano. The tranquility of the piano calmed my mind. I felt bliss.

I turned all the lights out and had candles burning in mason jars throughout my apartment. My shadow glided along the ceiling, the walls and floor as I went through each of my cabinets. I was looking for every prescription medication bottle I had. So far, I laid one bottle on the countertop of my bathroom vanity. I knew I had more. I needed more.

Three more bottles hiding in the back of my white lingerie dresser. Four bottles total. I refilled my glass of red wine and made my way back into the bathroom. I had all that I needed to get me through the last night of my existence.

Glancing in the mirror again I had to remind myself, *you want this.* I took another drink of my red wine and opened the first bottle of medication, etrafon. A medication my primary care physician prescribed to help me with my depression and anxiety.

It helped in the beginning, but after a while my body grew accustomed to it and it no longer worked.

Taking the first pill was easy. I placed it in my mouth and washed it down with the glass of red wine in my hand. *You did it*, I thought, *you did it*! I took another pill and another pill. Soon the bottle was empty, and I reached down for the next one, escitalopram.

Holding the bottle in my hand I paused for a minute. A rush of adrenaline worked through my veins. My pulse was racing. My heart beating faster than a drum. *Another drink of wine,* I said, and I opened the second bottle, pouring out all the pills in my hand. One quick swallow with a gulp of the wine and it was done.

I took a breath to let it all settle in. My stomach wanted to throw up, but I wouldn't let it. My knees felt weak beneath me. I began sweating and felt a daze coming on. I let the faucet run until the water was ice cold and then splashed it in my face. The coolness ran down my skin and rejuvenated me for a second. I didn't know if I could make it through a third bottle.

Don't give up now, I repeated to myself in the mirror. *You're nearly to the home stretch.*

Popping the top off the third bottle, rizatriptan, I emptied the two pills rattling at the bottom. I opened the fourth bottle, nortriptylin, and it was completely full. *Oh, thank God,* I murmured and started putting the pills in my mouth.

It took me a little while to get through the last bottle. I felt myself choking as red wine dripped out of the corners of my mouth. I began to gag, but I put my hands over my lips and breathed calmly through my nose. All done. Four different kinds of medications boiling inside of me. Now the waiting begins.

I could hear the thunder outside and I wanted to see it one last time. I put on my shawl, poured myself another glass of red wine and walked towards my back balcony. I wanted to breathe in the cool air and smell the rain as it fell. I wanted to hear the thunder growl and see the lightning strike as it lit up the night sky.

Nestling into my oversized patio chair, I felt the breeze from the light wind as it swirled around me. The view before me would be my last and it was mesmerizing. The world around me was still and for the first time in a long time, my mind was quiet. It was liberating.

How long were you sitting there, you may wonder, but I wouldn't know. I didn't have a clock in my view. I didn't care to. I wasn't timing how long it took me to die. It didn't seem like long though.

A numbness ran up my arms and legs. The red wine slipped from my hand and it fell to the concrete floor, shattering the glass completely. I heard the noise. It was a sharp piercing to my head, but I didn't want to move. I couldn't move. I was frozen.

My breathing was becoming faint. I could barely hear it anymore. My eyes were glossed over and everything turned into a blur. My head was spinning. As if I were on one of those merry-go-round rides at a kid's carnival. Going around and around and waiting patiently to get off; but this ride, I didn't want to get off.

I could feel my soul trying to leave my body. I wanted it to leave because that would have meant that I was dead. That I successfully ended my life. That I was leaving this world once and for all.

My eyelids started to droop. The world was fading fast from my view. I couldn't hear the thunder anymore. I couldn't hear anything. Then at last, my eyes shut and never reopened. I was still breathing though, but hardly. I felt a gasp of air in my lungs and it reached my mouth to come out, but nothing came back in. That was it. It was all over. I wasn't waking back up.

There was no one there to save me from my suicide. No one was with me. No one saw or heard or tried to stop me. I was there lying, slumped back in my chair with a life that was no longer there inside. I had completed my mission and the battle of suicide was finally over.

Would you have stepped in?

Would you have begged I think twice before doing this?

What is it that you would have done or said to me in that single moment?

The next morning as the sun began to rise, I was awakened to the sounds of car doors slamming shut and the engines starting. The red wine that had slipped from my hands last night had stained the patio concrete. *I failed at my own suicide,* I said. *One thing I try to do and I can't even do it right?* A groan came from my mouth as I got up and walked over to the balcony banister.

The morning air was fresh and a light fogginess was settled above the grass. The rays from the sun were gleaming on my skin. It was like heaven was shining all around. I smiled that my soul hadn't been another victim to the "S" word, and that I was given another chance at life. It was truly a beautiful morning. *Maybe there's a reason why I'm still alive,* I wondered. *Oh well,* I thought and turned around to go inside my apartment to take a shower. As I turned, my mouth dropped. Still in the patio chair, was my body. Lifeless.

You see, I was indeed dead, but somehow here I was standing right next to my own body. I don't know how or even why, but I was. *Is this what death does?* I thought. *You're dead, but you're still here at the same time?*

I ran off the balcony, through my apartment and downstairs. There was a woman walking to her car and I screamed, *Help! Please help me!* She didn't turn around. She didn't even flinch. She just kept walking. I got in here face, *Can you see me? Please tell me you can.* She couldn't. The woman walked right through me.

I was dead.

You think I would be happy, knowing that I didn't fail. That the "S" word had succeeded; but I wasn't. I was trembling with fear. I didn't understand how this could really be happening to me. *Am I a ghost now? What am I exactly?* I questioned.

Suddenly a familiar silver Ford Fusion pulled into a parking spot at my apartment.

PART 4
I Love You Alison

MOM! MOM! I yelled as loud as I could, *Mom, thank God you're here. You wouldn't believe what's hap--...* She couldn't hear me either. *M-m-mom,* I stuttered as she walked passed me. Nothing. She couldn't see me or feel me. She didn't know I killed myself. But I knew she must've sensed something was wrong since I didn't answer her call last night. I followed her up to my apartment, 1125B.

My tears started softly flowing because I knew she wouldn't be able to handle what she was about to find. My dead body. Digging in her purse, she searched to find the spare key I had given to her for emergencies. Crying I said, *Mom, please don't go in there. You don't want to see me like that.* Finding the spare key, she unlocked my front door and walked in.

"Alison," she said, "are you here? It's me, Mom. I was a little worried last night when - -". She paused. Looking around she noticed how spotless my apartment was. There wasn't a thing out of place. Mom knew something was wrong because I wasn't like that. I was messy. I hardly ever cleaned.

Mom went into my bedroom to see if I was still asleep, but she found a perfectly made bed.

She tried calling my cellphone again, but it went straight to my voicemail. Then she walked into my bathroom and turned on the lights. There, she saw my phone lying next to an empty bottle of red wine and all the prescription medication bottles. They were all empty as well. *I'm sorry Mom, I'm sorry.*

"Where are you Alison?" she asked herself, *"I don't understand."* I watched as she made her way to the front door. *Good,* I thought. I didn't want her finding me. Not her. Not like this. I always expected that someone else would find me. A neighbor that would notice they hadn't seen me in a couple of days or a coworker when I never came back to work. Someone other than my mom. She stopped. She looked behind her at the patio door and began walking toward it.

Turn the other way, Mom. Don't open the door. Please don't go out there, I screamed out. Mom didn't hear anything I was yelling out.

She opened the door and then she saw.

"Alison!" she ran over, shaking me. "Alison, wake up. Alison! Oh my God!" Her eyes swelling with tears. Lots of tears. "Come on baby girl. Wake up for Mamma. Come on. Oh Alison!" Mom pulled my body from the patio chair and checked my pulse. There wasn't one. She tilted my head back, cleared my airway and began doing mouth-to-mouth CPR and then chest compressions.

"Alison, come on. Come back to me. Baby, don't do this." She kept saying. But I couldn't. It had been nine hours since I died. I wasn't coming back. I was never coming back.

My spirit was broken for the pain my Mom was in. I fell at her side. Crying. She was crying. My body was in her arms and my head was against her chest and she slowly rocked me back and forth. I wanted to be in her warmth. To just feel her arms around me once again. I needed my Mom and she needed me too.

"It's okay Alison," she whispered, "it's okay. Mamma's here. I'm not going to leave you. You hear me? I'm never going to leave you." She kissed me on my forehead as her tears splashed onto my cheeks. "I love you Alison." She said. "With all my heart."

PART 5

The Whispers

THE PATH I chose has led me here to this point. I didn't think people cared about me. So this road was easier for me to walk. I honestly thought nobody would even take notice, but I was wrong. Standing in the midst of my own wake, I saw, and I listened.

What I assumed would be an audience of only my parents, turned into hundreds of people. My boss, my co-workers, friends, neighbors, some people I barely knew, the church, and all my family members. It was an astonishment for me to witness. It never even crossed my mind that I had people in my life who loved me.

"I don't get it. Were people unkind to her? Was I one of those people?" asked Norma.

"I never even suspected that anything was wrong. Did I miss a que?" asked Dale.

"I'm shocked! And I'm angry with myself. Maybe I could have done something if I had paid more attention than just being stuck in my own little world," said Jennifer.

"I can't wrap my mind around Alison killing herself. She never seemed like the type of person who would do something like this," said Wade.

"She was honest and kind. I never would've imagined she was dealing with suicide," said Chris.

"If I had known, I would have made sure she got the help and support she needed. I would've done something," said Elizabeth.

"I wish I would have said hello to her more often," said Rob.

"She was so smart! I loved having her as my manager. How could something like this happen?" asked Nancy.

"I don't have the words. My heart is truly broken for Alison and what she was going through. I'm sad she's gone, and I wish she was still here with us," said Alberta.

"I know there's nothing I can do now, but I'd give anything to change what happened to her," said Tina.

"I can't believe she's really gone," said Jillian. "Alison was such a beautiful person. She'd help anyone who needed it. Why didn't she let us know that now she needed help?" asked James.

"Come back. Please come back Alison," said Abigail.

"I shouldn't have kept canceling our lunch dates," said Katelyn.

"I remember her laugh. Nobody could laugh like her. I miss her so much," said Margaret.

"It doesn't seem real," said Thomas.

"Alison was a great human being. It doesn't make sense that she would kill herself," said Cathy.

"Did you know anything about this?" asked Phillip.

Walking among them, seeing their tears, hearing

their voices, I felt ashamed. So many people here to honor the memory of me and to support my family. Yet, there I was, lying in the casket. The guilt for what I had done was more than I could bare. I began to question if I had made the right decision a couple nights ago. Should I have ended my own life?

The room became smaller and the voices louder. My body didn't feel like my body anymore. I could see I was slowly fading, but not completely.

"I noticed she was acting a little quiet these past few weeks, but I didn't think much of it. I wish now I would've said something or asked if she were okay," said Ryan.

"I miss her," said Eleanor.

"This is tragic," said Reese.

"I'm stunned and I'm trying to understand, but I can't," said Hope.

"Was she depressed or anything? How come we didn't see the signs? I'm so upset this has happened," said Ruby.

"You don't think she was on anything do you? Like drugs?" said Jason.

"Was she lonely? I don't think she was dating or seeing anyone," said Amber.

Focus on the Beauty

A QUIET HUSH filled the sanctuary at First Baptist Church at the corner of 11th street and Hemingway. It was not a normal Saturday morning. For on this day, my parents, my family, friends, and everyone who knew me would gather in one place. Words would be spoken, tears would fall and the hymns of 'Amazing Grace' would be sung. It was a morning to tell me goodbye.

Pastor Morgan James held tightly to his bible as he made his way towards the pulpit. You could feel the sadness in his heart as he had been racking his mind these past few days, trying endlessly to understand my reasoning behind all this. He couldn't find the right answers he so desperately wanted. But he also knew that with suicide victims, sometimes, maybe all the time, the answers are never there to find.

Pastor James had been there in the very beginning to dedicate my life when I was a baby. He baptized me, counselled me and gave me encouragement as a teenager and young woman. He was truly a great man of God and I had always respected him for that. I didn't think about him when I committed suicide, that he too would be affected in such a mighty way.

Standing in front of the congregation, his heart grieving along with everyone else, I saw him look past my casket, to the stained-glass windows in the very back of the church. He knew that if he looked down and saw me, laying still and lifeless, he wouldn't be able to get through the speech he had prepared. The sobs coming from the people seated, echoed throughout the sanctuary. I felt every bit of pain and sorrow sitting in that sanctuary. I wanted to look away. To no longer see or hear, but I couldn't.

Clearing his throat, Pastor James began speaking.

"Today we are here to honor and remember the life of Alison Winters. A life that was ended too soon. I know we have many questions as we to try to understand this tragedy, but I want to take this moment and focus solely on the beauty of Alison's life. I'm reminded of her love for all people. How passionately she cared for others. She'd be the first one to give up all that she had to help someone around her. And it didn't even have to be someone she knew. Alison would help a perfect stranger because in her eyes, in her mind, she'd say with a smile, 'We're all just people who need someone.' Her heart was full of true kindness and generosity. She will be missed, but we shall never forget her memory.

We are also here in respect to her precious family. "Bill and Beth Winters, our hearts are here with you today in this time of deep sadness."

I know that in times like these, we can try to hide our emotions, but I want you to know that God himself said, 'Blessed are they that mourn: for they shall be comforted.' It's okay to breakdown and cry. To let go and allow ourselves to get lost in our tears because it's in these emotions that we find real comfort.

Death comes in all forms throughout this life and we try desperately to understand each situation. We want answers. We need them. Proverbs 3:5 says, 'Trust in the Lord with all thine heart; and lean not unto thine own understanding.' We must have trust in God. We must believe everything is going to be alright even though we don't understand or know that it will be.

I know we're all wondering if there was something that we could have done better or different to stop this from happening, but we cannot focus on that now. We need to ask ourselves, 'What is it that Alison wanted us to recognize from this?' Was it a simple hello? Or perhaps a small smile on our face? A stranger passing us by who sees us and takes notice instead of just walking on.

The greatest gift we can give to each other is love.

The time to love and to be kind is now.

Alison Winters was an example of this love, and it's up to us to spread her love. It's up to us to show this to the world."

Pastor James closed his bible and placed his hands on top of it. He asked everyone to bow their heads for a final prayer. A final goodbye.

Part 7

Lowering of Regrets

WALKING TO MY own grave site was haunting. I didn't want to be there. I could feel death. It was near me. It was very, very close. Silently it was calling out my name. *"Alison,"* it said, *"time is up."* It wanted me to follow. To rest. Forever.

I wanted to run away. I didn't want this to be the end. My final destination. The last chapter in my book. But it was. I let the "S" word in and it was the death of me.

You may ask, *What has changed your mind?* The answer is simple. When I was alive I sheltered myself. I kept my own distance. I cut myself off. I didn't allow myself to see the ones who were in front of me, behind me and next to me. The ones who cared about me, loved me and supported me. Those who wanted me to succeed in this life. The ones who are standing here now grieving my loss and honoring my memory. Those paying their respects one last time.

If I could take it all back, I would. If I could undo my suicide, I would. But I can't. I've already killed myself. I'm dead. And now, I'm about to be buried.

Four men carry my casket to the grave. They set me right above the dark hole that was previously dug. Slowly, inch by inch I'm lowered and with every inch comes with new regret.

The first lowering begins:

I can't be dead. This isn't what I wanted. I want

to be alive, to feel and to love. Can I go back? Just this once. I need to undo this mistake. I need to tell everyone, especially my parents that I was blind. I had everything I ever needed. All the things I'd been longing for, searching for; they were always there. I had everything because I had them in my life. I threw them all away because of the traps I set for myself. I killed myself. I did this. Why did I do this?

The second lowering:

I wish I had opened up and let you know that I was hurting. That I was losing sight of who I was, and I didn't know how to come back from the dark. I should've said something. Then maybe, just maybe, I'd still be alive with you.

The third lowering:

Collapsing in front of my own grave, I cried and cried. The "S" word destroyed not only me, but everyone else in my life. I fed into its power. I gave it life, because I quit. I listened to it and believed its lies. I stood by and watched as it killed me day by day. I did nothing. It stands over me still. It mocks me as my body lays cold in the closed casket. I'm more alone now than I ever thought I was when I was alive.

The forth lowering:

If I was given a second chance, I would take back that moment on Wednesday night. Suicide isn't the answer. It will never be the answer. You'll regret your decision as soon as you do it. I do. I regret all of it. I could warn them. I could stop them from doing this foolish act. You need to know. You need to understand all the life you're leaving behind. Everyone in your life will be affected.

I need to go back. I wish I could go back. I would tell you that once you're dead, that's it. You're dead. There's never any coming back from it. Your family won't ever get to see you again or hug you or call you up for no reason.

I would let you know that you're not alone. You must be strong enough to reach out and ask for help because people want to help. They do. I know. I've heard them say it.

The fifth lowering:

I'm nearly in the ground. I look back at my parents. Mom can't stop crying. Dad's buried his face in his hands as he sobs endlessly. It's breaking my heart to see the pain I've caused them. I know they don't understand what's going on or what was happening in my little world. If there was a way, I'd take all of their pain. I love them so much and I want to be alive now, so I can tell them. I'd run to them and tell them how sorry I am.

The sixth lowering:

I've run out of time. My casket has reached the bottom and death's face is staring at me. *Leave me alone,* I tell death. *Go away!* But it keeps staring. It never looks away from me. The first shovel of dirt hits my casket. Then another and another. *Don't bury me,* I scream. *Stop throwing dirt on me. I'm here.* The terror inside my voice scares me even more. But not a soul can hear anything I say.

I feel the suffocation from the dirt that surrounds me. I can't breathe or move. *Help me,* I breathlessly say, *don't bury me alive.* Please don't.

I am guilty of battling suicidal thoughts. For acting on those thoughts. I am guilty for taking my own life. I allowed suicide to creep up on me, plant itself, and grow deep inside me. I am guilty. Me, and me alone.

PART 8
The Letter

IT WAS NEARLY midnight when Mrs. Stevens, my parent's nextdoor neighbor left their house. My dad closed the front door, turned the lock and slowly began walking towards the kitchen to where my mom was. She was frantically putting away dishes. Mom wasn't good at goodbyes or letting go. Especially me, her only daughter.

My dad put his hand on her shoulder and said, "Beth, let it be. Dishes can wait until tomorrow." But she couldn't. She was literally falling apart on the inside from my suicide, and I feared the worst. I broke her heart and I never even meant to.

"Bill," she began, "I-I-I don't know, I can't. What am I supposed to do now? My baby - our baby is dead! She's lying in the ground right now! And why? How come? Did we not love her enough? What was happening in her life that was so terrible she felt she couldn't come to us. We didn't even get to say good-bye. She was alone. She died alone. Why? Did she know that we loved her and were proud of her? I feel like I'm dreaming because this can't be real. Bill, it can't be! It just can't be! Tell me I'm dreaming! Oh, God! Alison! Why did you do this? Why?" My mom's face was beat red from all the screaming and she fell into my dad's arms sobbing.

He tried to hold back the tears, to be strong for my mom, but a tear slipped out and then they just started pouring from his eyes. "We'll get through this, Beth," his voice breaking up, "Somehow. I don't know all the answers, but somehow, we'll get through this, together."

As my dad stood there, holding my mom, he glanced over and saw the mail that had piled up over the last couple of days. Something caught his eye. A handwritten letter addressed to them. Wiping his tears, he moved closer. His hands trembling as he reached down to pick up my letter.

With their hearts beating fast, my parents sat down at the kitchen table. Together they opened my letter:

Mom and Dad,

If you're reading this, it's because I'm dead. I know right now you're hurting, you're confused, and you don't know why I did what I did. I'm sorry. I'm sorry for the pain I'm causing you both. It was never my intention to make you sad or go out of your minds, trying to figure out if this was somehow your fault. It wasn't. You two are not to blame for the choice I've made. This was my choice. Mine. All mine.

I don't know if I can even begin to explain how I

feel because I can't seem to feel much of anything anymore. I'm in a battle; no, a war with myself. I can't think. I can't sleep. I'm lucky to just make it through my days. My soul has been searching for purpose, but I can't find it. I don't know what my purpose is anymore or what it is that I can contribute to this world. I've tried to find some sort of solitude, but it only brings me back to this moment right here. I didn't want it coming to this, but I can't seem to find another option. Ending my life is what my heart is desiring. In that, I have a peace inside of me. For knowing that my body will be at an eternal rest. No longer having the worries of this world anymore. No more fighting. No more battles. No more wars raging inside my mind.

I love you both so much and I always will.

All my love,
Alison